AF668425

THE STORY OF RĀMA

PART I

The Editors wish to acknowledge the role played by David Stollar and other members of the St James School Sanskrit faculty in the preparation of the material for the Sanskrit Course.

THE STORY OF RĀMA

A Sanskrit Coursebook For Beginners

Edited by

WARWICK JESSUP

ELENA JESSUP

PART I

MOTILAL BANARSIDASS PUBLISHERS
PRIVATE LIMITED • DELHI

Reprint : Delhi, 2016
First Indian Edition : Delhi, 2012
First Edition: London, 1997 (2001, 2005)

Published under arrangements with
St. James School,
Sanskrit Department, London

© 2005 by St. James Publishing
ALL RIGHTS RESERVED

ISBN : 978-81-208-3550-4 (PB Part I)
ISBN : 978-81-208-3551-1 (PB Part II)

MOTILAL BANARSIDASS
41 U.A. Bungalow Road, Jawahar Nagar, Delhi 110 007
8 Mahalaxmi Chamber, 22 Bhulabhai Desai Road, Mumbai 400 026
203 Royapettah High Road, Mylapore, Chennai 600 004
236, 9th Main III Block, Jayanagar, Bengaluru 560 011
8 Camac Street, Kolkata 700 017
Ashok Rajpath, Patna 800 004
Chowk, Varanasi 221 001

Printed using Times, Marking-RomanTM (transliteration) and SanskritpadaTM fonts designed and distributed by 6H Software, London (Tel. 020-8944 9496); © 1993-4 6H Software.

COVER DRAWING: Rāma

Printed in India

by RP Jain at NAB Printing Unit,
A-44, Naraina Industrial Area, Phase I, New Delhi–110028
and published by JP Jain for Motilal Banarsidass Publishers (P) Ltd.,
41 U.A. Bungalow Road, Jawahar Nagar, Delhi-110007

Foreword

by Prof Dr Satya Vrat Shastri

After a thorough perusal of these text books written by teachers of St James Schools in London for the teaching of Sanskrit, I am convinced of their utility for Indian schools. They are well-graded and supported by appropriate illustrations that make them very attractive to learners, particularly the young.

Today many Indian universities offer Sanskrit as an optional subject, even for those who are majoring in other subjects. For these students the books would be very effective in introducing them to Sanskrit which they might not have studied previously. The books could also be useful for those involved in performing arts like dance and music, or for students of Yoga and Ayurveda, subjects which have many Sanskrit references.

The first group of books entitled Sanskrit is Fun (3 volumes) introduce the learners to the Devanagari alphabet grouping the letters according to their place of articulation. Each group is given a designation, 'Family'. The 'Family' comprises both the vowels and the consonants. The learners are first taught how to draw the letters. The teaching is also helped by the humorous presentation of them in the form of animal figures. The next step is to add vowels to the consonants and then to teach joint consonants. Finally words and sentences are formed.

The second group of books seek to teach Sanskrit with reference to age-old stories of Krishna (2 volumes) and Rama (2 volumes). These stories with perennial interest of their own are then pressed into service to teach vocabulary, the formation of nouns and the conjugation of verbs in all three tenses. Adjectives and prepositions are also covered .

By the time learners have completed these books it is expected they would have a good basic grasp of the Sanskrit language, its vocabulary, structure and grammar. These books are an attempt to teach Sanskrit in a simple and systematic way that may well dispel the notion that Sanskrit is a difficult language.

Dr Shastri is currently an Honorary Professor at the Special Centre for Sanskrit Studies, Jawaharlal Nehru University, New Delhi. He was the Head of the Department of Sanskrit and the Dean of the Faculty of Arts at the University of Delhi, where he was the Pandit Manmohan Nath Dar Professor of Sanskrit (1970–1995).

Contents – Part One

	Page
Preface	x
Introduction	xi
Notes for Teachers/Students	xii
Definitions and Reminders	xiv
How the Story of the Rāmāyaṇa Came to be Told	xvi
Who was Vālmīki?	xvii

INTRODUCTORY EXERCISES 1

The Singular Forms of रामः	1
Exercises 1 and 2	2
भवति – The Present Time Singular	3
Exercise 3	3
New Words for the First Story	4

STORY – King Daśaratha Kills a Boy by Mistake **5**

भवति – All the Present Time Forms	8
Exercise 4	8
Exercise 5	9
Writing Sanskrit with English Letters	9
Exercises 6 and 7	10
Full Stops in Sanskrit	10
The Use of इति after Speech	11
Exercise 8	11
The 'Done To'	12
Exercise 9	12
Exercise 10	13
New Words for the Next Story	13

CHAPTER 2 14

STORY – Rāma and Lakṣmaṇa Kill the Demoness Tāṭakā **14**

The Future Time of भवति	17
Exercise 11	17
Exercise 12	18
The Past Time of भवति	18
Exercises 13 and 14	19
Agreement	20
Exercise 15	21
New Words for the Next Story	21

CHAPTER 3 22

STORY – Rāma Wins Sītā as his Wife	**22**
The Dual Forms of रामः	25
Exercise 16	25
Exercise 17	26
Writing Sanskrit with English Letters	26
Exercises 18 and 19	27
New Words for the Next Story	28

CHAPTER 4 29

STORY – The Cruel Kaikeyī Demands her Two Wishes	**29**
All the Forms of Rāma	33
The Endings for All Masculines in -अः	34
Exercises 20 and 21	35
The -त्वा Ending	36
Exercises 22 and 23	38
Writing Sanskrit with English Letters	39
Exercise 24	39
Exercises 25 and 26	40
The Crossword Puzzle	41
Clues to the Crossword Puzzle	42
New Words for the Next Story	43

CHAPTER 5 44

STORY – Rāvaṇa's Sister is Mutilated by Lakṣmaṇa	**44**
The Forms of मित्रम्	48
Exercises 27 and 28	49
Exercises 29 and 30	50
Writing Sanskrit with English Letters	51
Exercise 31	51
Exercises 32 and 33	52
Exercise 34	53
New Words for the Next Story	53

CHAPTER 6 54

STORY – Mārīca's Magic Helps Rāvaṇa Kidnap Sītā	**54**
The Forms of सीता	58
Exercises 35 and 36	59
Exercises 37 and 38	60

Writing Sanskrit with English Letters	61
Exercises 39 and 40	62
Exercises 41 and 42	63
सह with the Third Ending	64
Exercise 43	64
Exercise 44	65
New Words for the Next Story	65
CHAPTER 7	66
STORY – Rāvaṇa Cuts Off Jaṭāyu's Wings	**66**
The Neuter Forms of तत्	70
Exercise 45	71
The Masculine Forms of तत्	72
Exercises 46 and 47	73
Exercises 48 and 49	74
तत् Can also Describe a Noun	75
Exercise 50	75
Exercises 51 and 52	76
Exercise 53	77
Writing Sanskrit with English Letters	77
Exercises 54 and 55	78
Exercise 56	79
New Words for the Next Story	79
CHAPTER 8	80
STORY – Rāma, Grieving for Sītā, Finds Jaṭāyu Dying	**80**
The Feminine Forms of तत्	83
Exercises 57 and 58	84
Using the 6th Ending to Say 'Have'	85
Exercise 59	86
Exercise 60	87
Writing Sanskrit with English Letters	87
Exercises 61 and 62	88
Exercises 63 and 64	89
APPENDICES	90
1. Verses to Recite	91
2. Writing Sanskrit with English Letters	94
3. Summary of Word Forms	99
4. Vocabulary: English–Sanskrit	108
5. Vocabulary: Sanskrit–English	117

Preface

by Professor Richard Gombrich

It is a privilege for me to be invited to introduce this set of textbooks. They have been compiled with loving care by the teachers of the Sanskrit Department of St James School in London. Their slow birth reflects the years of teaching experience which have gone into their making.

Sanskrit is by no means an easy language: even in India it is mastered only by a small minority of the population. The grammar is complicated, even if someone who masters it will finally discover that it is more systematic and less irregular than that of English. The vocabulary is vast, reflecting the vast span of time and geographical area over which Sanskrit has been used. Learning to read and write an Indian script is also a major undertaking for a student from another culture. (Luckily for us Europeans, at least it is written left to write and top to bottom.)

On the other hand, Sanskrit is not only a beautiful language written in a beautiful script; it is the vehicle of classical Indian culture, the culture which has given the world one of its greatest literatures and greatest civilizations. Sanskrit achieved something not very different from the form it still has today more than three thousand years ago. The reason why it has survived so well, and may well outlive most of the languages which the world is now using, is not hard to understand: it is because of the aesthetic attractions and the intellectual and spiritual value of the content of so many Sanskrit texts.

Only a few students are likely to have the opportunity to go on to study Sanskrit in depth, so that they can enjoy reading Sanskrit by themselves. There will be so many rival claims on their attention. But even those who only work through these books are likely to look back on the experience with satisfaction, a feeling that they have done something truly worth while. And the few who go further will be grateful that these books have launched them on an unforgettable experience.

Prof Gombrich was the Boden Professor of Sanskrit at the University of Oxford from 1976 to 2004 and was a past President of the Pali Text Society (1994–2002) and General Editor Emeritus of the Clay Sanskrit Library. He is currently the Boden Professor of Sanskrit Emeritus, University of Oxford

Introduction to the Sanskrit Language

Language is fundamental to a human being. For this reason, it is a primary element in education. Language is one of the greatest gifts that a student is given. How a person learns to speak is all important and will be determined by example. So the aim of the teacher should be to present the student with the finest language.

Linguists agree that one of the finest languages is Sanskrit. Sir William Jones, recognised as a founder of modern linguistics, said in 1786:

> "The Sanskrit language, whatever be its antiquity, is of a wonderful structure; more perfect than the Greek, more copious than the Latin, and more exquisitely refined than either; yet bearing to both of them a stronger affinity, both in the roots of verbs and the forms of grammar, than can possibly have been produced by accident."

The considerable benefits of studying the classical languages, Greek and Latin, have been known in the West for hundreds of years; indeed, in recent centuries some of the best education available in the world has been based upon them. However, Sir William Jones had discovered a classical language *par excellence,* more ancient than Greek or Latin, which had been preserved intact for thousands of years.

The word 'Sanskrit' means 'perfected', for its sound system and grammar are scientifically structured. It has even been put forward as being the most suitable language for use in computers (see 'Knowledge Representation in Sanskrit and Artificial Intelligence', *The A.I. Magazine,* Spring 1985).

Sanskrit also has one of the greatest literatures known to humanity. The Sanskrit epics, the *Rāmāyaṇa* and the *Mahābhārata,* are inspiring and fascinating. Readers of all ages love these stories and enjoy the company of great and heroic men and women.

Notes for Teachers/Students

THE COURSE

This book follows on from *The Stories of Krishna* (Part Two), and has been designed for elementary students. *The Stories of Krishna* (Parts One and Two) cover:

- full declensions of the most common type of masculine, feminine and neuter nouns;
- conjugations of a simple verb in present, future and past times; and
- twelve stories based on the childhood of Krishna.

The present volume is the first of two parts of *The Story of Rāma,* which together relate in 16 episodes the story of the *Rāmāyaṇa*. Part One contains the first eight stories. It begins with a revision of the grammar learned in the *The Stories of Krishna* books, and then goes on to introduce:

- the standard method of transliteration of the Sanskrit script;
- the gerund ('having done something');
- various Sanskrit idioms; and
- the declension of the Sanskrit word for 'that' in all three genders.

WRITING

At this stage those pupils who have mastered writing the Sanskrit script beautifully with a pencil could be taught how to use a Sanskrit pen.

STORIES

Before teaching this book, the teacher should be familiar with the story of the *Rāmāyaṇa*. Although summaries of the plot are included in the text, a fund of background knowledge of the detail of the *Rāmāyaṇa* is invaluable.

Before a new story is begun, the new words for that story should be practised orally over the course of several lessons, and the students tested.

Following this, each student should in turn be asked to read each sentence aloud and give an oral translation for each sentence. When an appropriate section of the story has been completed orally, the students should write their own translation in an exercise book.

Not every student will complete the whole of every story or exercise. Once the teacher judges it right to move on, the class should do so.

TEXTS FOR RECITATION

Appendix 1 to this volume comprises a small selection of suggested Sanskrit texts which students could recite on a daily basis. It has been found that this often enhances the student's experience of the beauty of the language and of its fluent pronunciation. The selection is, of course, only a sample of what can be found. Students may wish to add some of their own favourite texts.

OTHER DETAILS

Regular practice of all the noun declensions and of the conjugations of verbs so far covered needs to continue as the course proceeds.

The Story of Rāma (Parts One and Two) together should take about four or five terms to complete.

Note to teachers/students: To be revised orally. It would be useful briefly to revise and test these definitions and grammatical concepts prior to embarking on the chapters that follow.

DEFINITIONS AND REMINDERS

1. A noun is **a name** (e.g., David, school, राम).
2. An adjective tells **the quality of something** (e.g., white, विशाल°).
3. A verb is **an action** (e.g., he walks, I saw, खादति).
4. The First Ending shows **the doer** of the action (e.g., रामः, सीता).
5. The Vocative shows **the person called** (e.g., हे राम, O king).
6. The Second Ending shows **the thing done to** (e.g., रामम्, सीताम्).
7. The Third Ending means **'by'** (e.g., रामेण, सीतया).
8. The Fourth Ending means **'for'** (e.g., रामाय, सीतायै).
9. The Fifth Ending means **'from'** (e.g., रामात्, सीतायाः).
10. The Sixth Ending means **'of'** (e.g., रामस्य, सीतायाः).
11. The Seventh Ending means **'in'** (e.g., रामे, सीतायाम्).

1. Nouns in Sanskrit are masculine, feminine or neuter (e.g., रामः, सीता, मित्रम्).
2. Nouns in Sanskrit have special endings for one, two or many.
3. In Sanskrit sentences the verb usually goes at the end.
4. A verb may speak of three times: past, present or future.
5. A verb may speak of three persons:
(i) he, she, it or they;
(ii) you; or
(iii) I or we.
6. 'Agreement' is where the ending of the adjective has a similar ending to the noun. It has the same number (i.e., singular, dual or plural), the same gender (i.e., masculine, feminine or neuter), and the same type of ending (i.e., First, Second, Third, etc.).
7. The ending of a verb agrees in number with the doer or doers of the action.

How the Story of the Rāmāyaṇa Came to be Told

The sage Vālmīki asked the great Nārada: 'Who in this world is a true hero?' Nārada told Vālmīki the story of the life of Rāma.

After hearing Nārada, Vālmīki wandered in the forest, and saw a bird shot by a hunter. A beautiful Sanskrit verse sprang to his lips as he grieved for the dying bird.

Vālmīki passed into deep meditation, and came face to face with the Creator. The Creator asked Vālmīki to let the whole of the story of Rāma be spoken in such beautiful verses, for the good of the world.

Vālmīki spoke forth twenty-four thousand Sanskrit verses, then taught them to the sons of Rāma and Sītā, Kuśa and Lava. The two princes sang the whole story in Sanskrit beautifully from memory in front of Rāma himself.

Vālmīki approaches Nārada, who tells him the story of Rāma. Vālmīki then tells the story to us.

Who was Vālmīki ?

Vālmīki was a robber. He used to stop people on the road, kill them, and take their money.

Once Vālmīki stopped a wise man. The wise man told Vālmīki that his evil deeds would cause him to suffer great misery in the future.

Vālmīki asked for the wise man's help.

The wise man told Vālmīki to repeat the name of Rāma in his mind again and again. Vālmīki did this, and became so entranced that he sat for a long time in one place, thinking only on Rāma's name.

While he sat there, ants made an ant-hill on top of him. The Sanskrit for 'ant-hill' is *'valmīka'*, and this is how he received his name.

By repeating the name of Rāma, Vālmīki became a sage.

Introductory Exercises

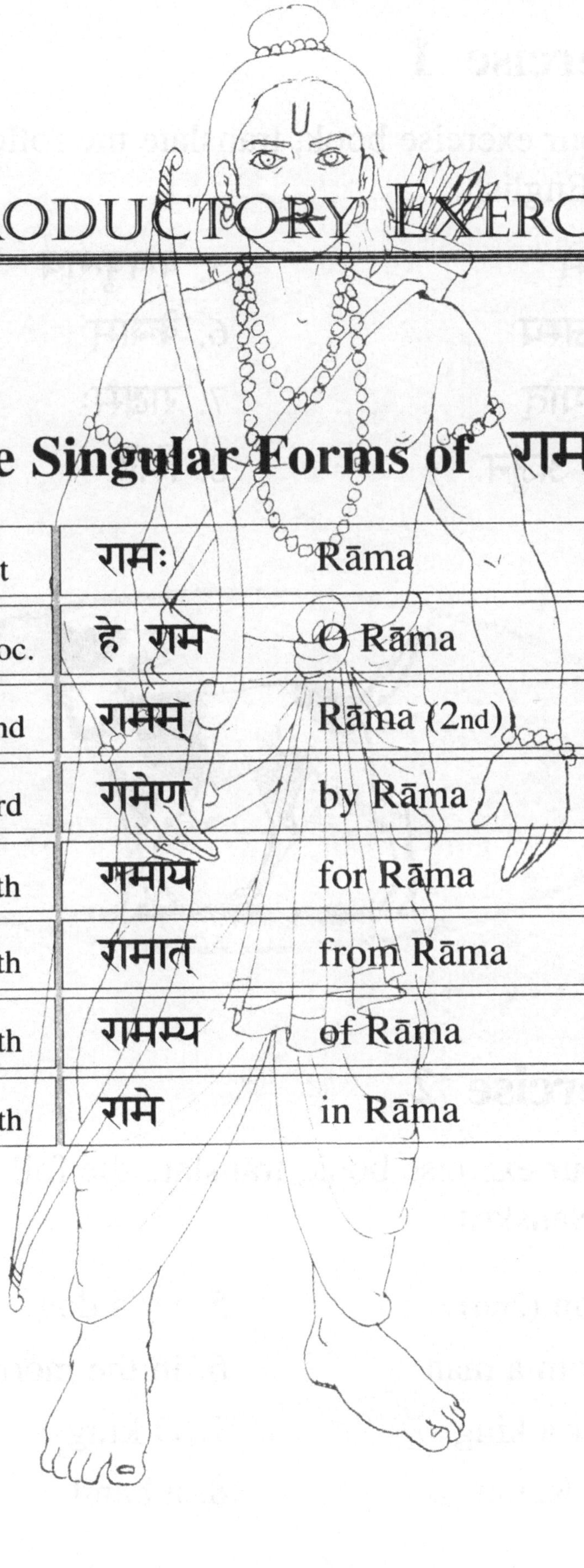

The Singular Forms of रामः

1st	रामः	Rāma
Voc.	हे राम	O Rāma
2nd	रामम्	Rāma (2nd)
3rd	रामेण	by Rāma
4th	रामाय	for Rāma
5th	रामात्	from Rāma
6th	रामस्य	of Rāma
7th	रामे	in Rāma

Exercise 1

In your exercise book, translate the following into English.

1. रामे
2. गजस्य
3. खगात्
4. हे अर्जुन
5. कुक्कुराय
6. केशम्
7. राक्षसः
8. सिंहे

Exercise 2

In your exercise book, translate the following into Sanskrit.

1. lion (2nd)
2. from a man
3. for a king
4. in Rāma
5. by a dog
6. in the moon
7. O king
8. a hand

भवति – The Present Time Singular

First Person	भवति	he becomes
Middle Person	भवसि	you become
Best Person	भवामि	I become

Exercise 3

In your exercise book, translate the following into English.

1. भवति
2. भवामि
3. पिबामि
4. पश्यसि
5. पश्यति
6. भवसि
7. पिबति
8. पश्यामि

New Words for the Next Story

दशरथः	Daśaratha	तस्मात्	therefore
शब्दः	sound	शोकः	grief
चिन्तयति	thinks	अहम्	I
शरः	arrow	त्वम्	you
क्षिपति	shoots	अपि	also
बालकः	boy	भविष्यसि	you will become
जनकः	father		

Chapter One

STORY

King Daśaratha Kills a Boy by Mistake

Vālmīki says:

"King Daśaratha, when a boy, goes hunting in the forest at night time. Hearing the sound of gurgling water, he thinks an elephant is drinking. He shoots his arrow off in the direction of the sound, but then discovers he has shot a boy who was collecting water for his blind father. Daśaratha carries the body of the boy to the father. The father, dying of grief, puts a curse on Daśaratha that he too would die of grief for a son."

[for the story in Sanskrit, see page 7]

King Daśaratha shoots his arrow.

[continued from page 5]

[The following story should first be read aloud around the class. The pupils should then copy out the sentences one at a time. Beneath each Sanskrit word should be written its English meaning. On a third line the pupils should write a translation of the whole sentence. In subsequent stories this procedure can be followed, or on occasions the students can be asked simply to translate the story into English without writing out the Sanskrit. Self-study students should adapt the exercises accordingly.]

The story in Sanskrit:

King Daśaratha

1. नृपः अस्ति।
2. नृपः दशरथः नाम।
3. दशरथः वनम् गच्छति।
4. चन्द्रः गगने भाति।
5. दशरथः जलस्य शब्दम् शृणोति।
6. गजः पिबति इति दशरथः चिन्तयति।
7. दशरथः शरम् क्षिपति।
8. शरः तु बालकम् व्यापादयति।
9. दशरथः बालकस्य जनकम् गच्छति।
10. बालकस्य जनकः वदति।
11. अहम् शोकात् मृतः भवामि।
12. तस्मात् त्वम् अपि शोकात् मृतः भविष्यसि इति॥

भवति – All the Present Time Forms

	SINGULAR	*DUAL*	*PLURAL*
First Person	भवति he, she, it becomes	भवतः they two become	भवन्ति they many become
Middle Person	भवसि you become	भवथः you two become	भवथ you many become
Best Person	भवामि I become	भवावः we two become	भवामः we many become

Exercise 4

In your exercise book, translate the following into English.

1. भवति
2. पिबन्ति
3. चिन्तयथ
4. पतसि
5. गच्छामः
6. हसतः
7. चरामि
8. खादथ
9. क्षिपसि
10. गच्छावः

Exercise 5

In your exercise book, translate the following into Sanskrit.

1. I become.
2. You become.
3. He hits.
4. They two go.
5. I eat.
6. He goes.
7. We many think.
8. You two bow.
9. We two fall.
10. He speaks.

Writing Sanskrit with English Letters

The first rule is that long vowels are written with a bar over them. Here are some Sanskrit vowels which are written using English letters.

अ *is written* a		आ *is written* ā	
इ *is written* i		ई *is written* ī	
उ *is written* u		ऊ *is written* ū	
ऋ *is written* ṛ		ॠ *is written* ṝ	

Exercise 6

In your exercise book, write the following Sanskrit letters using English letters.

1. अ
2. ऊ
3. इ
4. आ
5. उ

Exercise 7

In your exercise book, write the following in Sanskrit.

1. a
2. ṝ
3. ī
4. ṛ
5. u

Full Stops in Sanskrit

An upright bar marks the end of a sentence (।).
A double bar marks the end of a longer passage (॥).

The Use of इति after Speech

In a Sanskrit story, when something has been said or thought, the word इति is added to mark where the speech or thought ends. This is like writing speech marks after speech. इति can be translated as 'thus'. For example:

रामः नगरम् गच्छति इति सीता अवदत् ॥
"Rāma is going to the city", thus said Sītā.

Exercise 8

Translate into English, giving a word-for-word, then a complete, translation:

1. रामः गच्छति इति सीता वदति।
2. गजः पिबति इति दशरथः चिन्तयति।
3. शोकात् मृतः भवामि इति दशरथः वदति।
4. रामः सीताम् अवदत् लक्ष्मणः धावति इति।
5. नारी नरम् वदति रामम् पश्यामि इति।

The 'Done To'

Remember that the Second Ending of a word shows the thing 'done to'. Words which have the Second Ending end in 'अम्' like रामम्.

Example:

नरः	रामम्	पश्यति ।
man	Rāma (2nd)	sees

The man sees Rāma.

Exercise 9

In your exercise book, translate the following Sanskrit sentences into English. For each sentence write the Sanskrit first, then a word-for-word translation, then finally a full translation.

1. रामः नरम् पश्यति ।
2. रामम् नरः पश्यति ।
3. खगः मत्स्यम् गच्छति ।
4. मत्स्यम् खगः गच्छति ।
5. कुक्कुरः वृक्षम् धावति ।

Exercise 10

In your exercise book, translate the following English sentences into Sanskrit.

1. The demon eats the man.
2. Daśaratha sees the moon.
3. The king goes to the chariot.
4. The lion drinks the water.

New Words for the Next Story

रामः	Rāma	ताटका	Tāṭakā
सोदरः	brother	घोर°	horrible
लक्ष्मणः	Lakṣmaṇa	कर्णः	ear
आचार्यः	teacher	सुखित°	happy
विश्वामित्रः	Viśvāmitra		

Chapter Two

STORY

The Cruel Kaikeyī Demands Her Two Wishes

Vālmīki says:

"King Daśaratha's sons, Rāma and Lakṣmaṇa, go off to the forest with their teacher, Viśvāmitra. They meet a demoness called Tāṭakā. Lakṣmaṇa cuts off Tāṭakā's nose and ears, and Rāma finally kills her with an arrow. The forest people are happy."

The story in Sanskrit:

1. दशरथस्य पुत्रः रामः नाम।
2. रामस्य सोदरः लक्ष्मणः नाम।
3. रामस्य आचार्यः विश्वामित्रः नाम।

[continues on page 16]

Viśvāmitra watches as Rāma and Lakṣmaṇa prepare to kill Tāṭakā.

[continued from page 14]

4. रामः लक्ष्मणः विश्वामित्रः च वनम् गच्छन्ति।
5. तत्र राक्षसी अस्ति।
6. राक्षसी ताटका नाम।
7. ताटकायाः रूपम् घोरम् अस्ति।
8. सा रक्तम् पिबति।
9. लक्ष्मणेन ताटकायाः नासिका छिन्ना भवति।
10. लक्ष्मणेन ताटकायाः कर्णौ अपि छिन्नौ भवतः।
11. रामस्य शरः ताटकायाः हृदयम् प्रविशति।
12. ताटका मृता भवति।
13. रामः लक्ष्मणः च जयतः।

The Future Time of भवति

	SINGULAR	*DUAL*	*PLURAL*
First Person	भविष्यति he, she, it will become	भविष्यतः they two will become	भविष्यन्ति they many will become
Middle Person	भविष्यसि you will become	भविष्यथः you two will become	भविष्यथ you many will become
Best Person	भविष्यामि I shall become	भविष्यावः we two shall become	भविष्यामः we many shall become

Exercise 11

In your exercise book, translate the following into English.

1. भविष्यसि
2. वदिष्यथ
3. चरिष्यावः
4. धाविष्यन्ति
5. खादिष्यति
6. भविष्यामि
7. पतिष्यतः
8. हसिष्यथः
9. चरिष्यामः
10. करिष्यति

Exercise 12

In your exercise book, translate the following into Sanskrit.

1. We many shall eat.
2. He will speak.
3. You many will fall.
4. I shall become.
5. They two will fall.
6. You many will run.
7. We two shall walk.
8. You two will laugh.
9. They many will do.
10. I shall fall.

The Past Time of भवति

	SINGULAR	*DUAL*	*PLURAL*
First Person	अभवत् he, she, it became	अभवताम् they two became	अभवन् they many became
Middle Person	अभवः you became	अभवतम् you two became	अभवत you many became
Best Person	अभवम् I became	अभवाव we two became	अभवाम we many became

Exercise 13

In your exercise book, translate the following into English.

1. अगच्छत्
2. अतुदः
3. अपिबत्
4. अचिन्तयम्
5. अखादाव
6. अपिबम्
7. अवदताम्
8. अभवन्
9. अहसत
10. अभवाम

Exercise 14

In your exercise book, translate the following into Sanskrit.

1. He laughed.
2. They two ate.
3. You spoke.
4. I became.
5. We many fell.
6. You two thought.
7. They many drank.
8. You many ran.
9. We two walked.
10. I spoke.

Agreement

An adjective tells the quality of something.
For example:

प्राज्ञ wise

The ending of an adjective must be the same as the word it goes with. If the noun is masculine, the ending of the adjective will also be masculine. For example:

प्राज्ञः नरः a wise man

Likewise, if the noun is speaking of one, two or many things, the ending of the adjective will agree. For example:

प्राज्ञौ नरौ two wise men

Finally, if the noun has a First Ending, the adjective will also have a First Ending. If the noun has a Fourth Ending, the adjective will also have a Fourth Ending. For example:

प्राज्ञाय नराय for a wise man

Exercise 15

- Copy the following into your exercise book.
- Then put the correct ending on the adjective so that it agrees with the noun that it tells us about.
- Finally, translate them both.

1. प्राज्ञ_ नृपः
2. सुखित_ सोदरम्
3. शुद्ध_ यशोदा
4. अभय_ नराः
5. घोर_ राक्षसान्
6. उत्तम_ नगरे
7. प्रथम_ बालकात्
8. नील_ गृहस्य

New Words for the Next Story

मिथिला	Mithilā (a city)	चापः	bow
जनकः	Janaka (a king)	यदि	if
कन्या	daughter	उद्धरति	lifts up
सीता	Sītā	उदहरत्	lifted up
रमणीय॰	beautiful	भार्या	wife
राजगृहम्	palace	अयोध्या	Ayodhyā (a city)
शिवः	Śiva		

Chapter Three

STORY

Rāma Wins Sītā as His Wife

Vālmīki says:

"Rāma goes to Mithilā. There King Janaka has a huge bow given by Śiva. King Janaka says that if Rāma is able to pick up and string the bow, he could have the hand of his beautiful daughter Sītā in marriage. Rāma not only lifts but breaks the bow, wins the hand of Sītā, and returns home to Ayodhyā."

The story in Sanskrit:

1. रामः मिथिलाम् अगच्छत्।
2. तत्र नृपः जनकः नाम।
3. जनकस्य कन्या सीता नाम।

[continues on page 24]

Rāma breaks Śiva's bow as Sītā and King Janaka watch.

[continued from page 22]

4. सा रमणीया कन्या।
5. जनकस्य राजगृहे शिवस्य चापः आसीत्।
6. जनकः अवदत् यदि रामः शिवस्य चापम् उद्धरिष्यति सीता तस्य भार्या भविष्यति इति।
7. रामः शिवस्य चापम् उदहरत्।
8. सीता रामस्य भार्या अभवत्।
9. रामः सीता च अयोध्याम् आगच्छताम्।
10. अयोध्यायाम् आनन्दः आसीत्॥

The city of Ayodhyā

The Dual Forms of रामः

1st	रामौ	two Rāmas
Voc.	हे रामौ	O two Rāmas
2nd	रामौ	two Rāmas (2nd)
3rd	रामाभ्याम्	by two Rāmas
4th	रामाभ्याम्	for two Rāmas
5th	रामाभ्याम्	from two Rāmas
6th	रामयोः	of two Rāmas
7th	रामयोः	in two Rāmas

Exercise 16

In your exercise book, translate the following into English.

1. रामाभ्याम्
2. चापयोः
3. खगाभ्याम्
4. हे लक्ष्मण
5. सिंहाय
6. कर्णौ
7. नृपः
8. बालके

Exercise 17

In your exercise book, translate the following into Sanskrit.

1. two lions (2nd)
2. from two boys
3. for two kings
4. in Rāma
5. by a dog
6. in two moons
7. O king
8. a hand

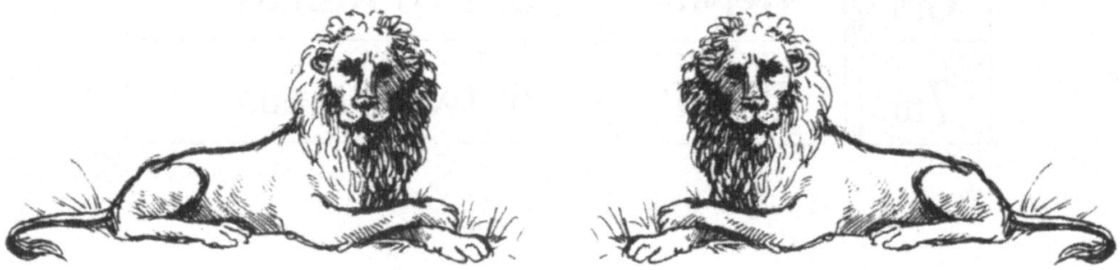

Writing Sanskrit with English Letters

Now we shall learn how to write
ए, ऐ, ओ and औ
using English letters.

ए *is written* e

ऐ *is written* ai

ओ *is written* o

औ *is written* au

Exercise 18

In your exercise book, write the following Sanskrit letters using English letters.

1. ए
2. आ
3. इ
4. ओ
5. ई
6. ऋ
7. ऐ
8. औ

Rāma takes the hand of Sītā.

Exercise 19

In your exercise book, write the following in Sanskrit.

1. a
2. ṛ
3. e
4. u
5. ai
6. au

New Words for the Next Story

तिस्रः	three (feminine)	वरः	wish
कौसल्या	Kausalyā	प्रार्थयति	asks for
सुमित्रा	Sumitrā	गमिष्यति	will go
कैकेयी	Kaikeyī	गच्छ	go!
भरतः	Bharata	अहम्	I
शत्रुघ्नः	Śatrughna		

King Daśaratha with his three wives – Kausalyā, Sumitrā and Kaikeyī

Chapter Four

STORY

The Cruel Kaikeyī Demands Her Two Wishes

Vālmīki says:

"Daśaratha has three wives and four sons. He intends his son, Rāma, to be king after him. Daśaratha previously gave his wife Kaikeyī two boons. She now claims them, saying that her son, Bharata, should be king, and that Rāma should go to the forest. Rāma goes to the forest, accompanied by his wife, Sītā, and his brother, Lakṣmaṇa. Daśaratha dies of grief.

The story in Sanskrit:

1. दशरथस्य तिस्रः भार्याः ।
2. भार्याः कौसल्या सुमित्रा कैकेयी नाम ।

[continues on page 31]

The cruel Kaikeyī demands her wishes.

[continued from page 29]

3. दशरथस्य पुत्राः रामः भरतः लक्ष्मणः शत्रुघ्नः नाम।
4. दशरथः अचिन्तयत् रामः मम उत्तमः पुत्रः।
5. अचिरेण रामः नृपः भविष्यति इति।
6. कैकेयी तु अचिन्तयत् मम भरतः नृपः भविष्यति इति।
7. वरौ ददामि इति दशरथः कैकेयीम् अवदत्।
8. कैकेयी अवदत् मम वरौ प्रार्थयामि।

[continues next page]

The four sons of King Daśaratha – Śatrughna, Rāma, Lakṣmaṇa and Bharata

[continued]

9. भरतः नृपः भविष्यति।
10. तदा रामः वनम् गमिष्यति इति।
11. कैकेयी रामम् अवदत् हे राम वनम् गच्छ इति।
12. सीता अवदत् अहम् अपि वनम् आगच्छामि इति।
13. लक्ष्मणः अवदत् अहम् अपि आगच्छामि इति।
14. रामः लक्ष्मणः सीता च वनम् अगच्छन्।
15. दशरथः शोकात् मृतः अभवत्॥

All the Forms of रामः

We shall now add the Plural forms of रामः alongside those of the Singular and the Dual.

SINGULAR	*DUAL*	*PLURAL*
रामः one Rāma	रामौ two Rāmas	रामाः many Rāmas
हे राम O Rāma	हे रामौ O two Rāmas	हे रामाः O many Rāmas
रामम् Rāma (2nd)	रामौ two Rāmas (2nd)	रामान् many Rāmas (2nd)
रामेण by Rāma	रामाभ्याम् by two Rāmas	रामैः by many Rāmas
रामाय for Rāma	रामाभ्याम् for two Rāmas	रामेभ्यः for many Rāmas
रामात् from Rāma	रामाभ्याम् from two Rāmas	रामेभ्यः from many Rāmas
रामस्य of Rāma	रामयोः of two Rāmas	रामाणाम् of many Rāmas
रामे in Rāma	रामयोः in two Rāmas	रामेषु in many Rāmas

The Endings for All Masculines in -अः

The endings for रामः are used with all masculine nouns ending in -अः. Here is another example, शरः (arrow).

SINGULAR	*DUAL*	*PLURAL*
शरः one arrow	शरौ two arrows	शराः many arrows
हे शर O arrow	हे शरौ O two arrows	हे शराः O many arrows
शरम् arrow (2nd)	शरौ two arrows (2nd)	शरान् many arrows (2nd)
शरेण by an arrow	शराभ्याम् by two arrows	शरैः by many arrows
शराय for an arrow	शराभ्याम् for two arrows	शरेभ्यः for many arrows
शरात् from an arrow	शराभ्याम् from two arrows	शरेभ्यः from many arrows
शरस्य of an arrow	शरयोः of two arrows	शराणाम् of many arrows
शरे in an arrow	शरयोः in two arrows	शरेषु in many arrows

Exercise 20

In your exercise book, translate the following into English. Give all possible translations.

1. रामाय
2. हस्तौ
3. वृक्षेषु
4. गजेभ्यः
5. खगानाम्
6. नृपस्य
7. हे सर्पौ
8. शरान्
9. शिवेन
10. वराभ्याम्

Exercise 21

In your exercise book, translate the following into Sanskrit.

1. from many birds
2. by many snakes
3. many chariots
4. for two men
5. by hand
6. in an elephant
7. of a lion
8. son (2nd)
9. O Rāma
10. for a dog

The -त्वा Ending

The -त्वा ending gives a sense of an action having been completed. It is often translated as 'having'. For example:

गत्वा having gone

The -त्वा word does not replace the main verb in the sentence. For example:

रथम्	गत्वा	सः	नृपम्	अपश्यत् ।
chariot (2nd)	having gone	he	king (2nd)	saw

Having gone to the chariot, he saw the king.

Here is a list of important -त्वा words alongside the verbs to which they are related.

VERBS		*RELATED -त्वा WORDS*	
शृणोति	hears	श्रुत्वा	having heard
गच्छति	goes	गत्वा	having gone
पश्यति	sees	दृष्ट्वा	having seen
नमति	bows	नत्वा	having bowed
भवति	becomes	भूत्वा	having become
करोति	does	कृत्वा	having done

Exercise 22

In your exercise book, translate the following Sanskrit sentences into English. For each sentence:

- first write the Sanskrit;
- then write a word-for-word translation;
- and finally write out a full translation.

1. नगरम् गत्वा नरः जलम् अपिबत् ।
2. खगम् श्रुत्वा नारी अहसत् ।
3. चन्द्रम् दृष्ट्वा रामः पुष्पम् सीतायै अददात् ।
4. नृपः भूत्वा सिंहः सुखितः अभवत् ।
5. खगः भूत्वा सः वृक्षात् अपतत् ।

Exercise 23

In your exercise book, translate the following into Sanskrit.

1. Having gone to the house, the man ate.
2. Having gone to the house, the man saw his son.
3. Having seen the moon, the lady thought.
4. Having become happy, the boy laughed.
5. Having heard the father, Rāma lifted the bow of Śiva.

Writing Sanskrit with English Letters

Now we shall learn how to write some Sanskrit consonants using English letters.

क	ka	च	ca	ट	ṭa	त	ta	प	pa
ख	kha	छ	cha	ठ	ṭha	थ	tha	फ	pha
ग	ga	ज	ja	ड	ḍa	द	da	ब	ba
घ	gha	झ	jha	ढ	ḍha	ध	dha	भ	bha

Exercise 24

In your exercise book, write the following Sanskrit letters using English letters.

1. क
2. झ
3. ड
4. ब
5. ढ
6. द
7. ट
8. घ

Exercise 25

In your exercise book, write the following in Sanskrit.

1. pha
2. ṭa
3. kha
4. ca
5. ḍa
6. ai

Exercise 26

In your exercise book, write the following Sanskrit words using English letters.

1. गज
2. खग
3. अघ
4. एक

The elephant isn't sure he can solve the Crossword Puzzle on the next page. Can YOU?

(See next page for clues.)

Clues to Crossword Puzzle

*Note to Teachers/Students: The puzzle should be completed in Sanskrit script.
A conjunct consonant occupies one square, as does a visarga.
1 across and 1 down are already filled in as examples.*

ACROSS

1. "रामः मम _____ पुत्रः" *(see page 31)*
2. a chariot
3. thinks
5. he will do
7. Ayodhyā and Mithilā are examples of this.
8. becomes
10. the hero of this book
11. O Rāma
13. "ताटकायाः _____ घोरम् अस्ति" *(see page 16)*
16. book
18. bows
19. he

DOWN

1. lifts up
3. a chin
4. "अयोध्यायाम् _____ आसीत्" *(see page 24)*
6. stands
9. a forest
10. by two Rāmas
12. a prince
14. falls
15. mother
17. a daughter

New Words for the Next Story

पर्णगृहम्	leaf-house	स्निह्यति	(+ 7th)	falls in love
गायति	sings	रावणः		Rāvaṇa
एकदा	once	शूर्पणखा		Śūrpaṇakhā
		तव		your

Rāvaṇa, king of the demons

Chapter Five

STORY

Rāvaṇa's Sister is Mutilated by Lakṣmaṇa

Vālmīki says:
"In the forest, Rāma, Sītā and Lakṣmaṇa live in a leaf-house. Śūrpaṇakhā, a demoness, asks Rāma to marry her. When refused, Śūrpaṇakhā threatens to eat Sītā. Lakṣmaṇa cuts off the demoness's nose and ears. Śūrpaṇakhā runs back to Rāvaṇa, her brother, king of the demons. Rāvaṇa resolves to destroy Rāma."

The story in Sanskrit:

1. वनम् गत्वा लक्ष्मणः रामाय पर्णगृहम् अकरोत् ।
2. वने खगाः वृक्षेषु अगायन् ।
3. सर्वम् रमणीयम् ।

[continues on page 46]

Rāma, Sītā and Lakṣmaṇa in the forest

[continued from page 44]

4. एकदा तु घोरा राक्षसी रामम् आगच्छत्।
5. सा रामे अस्निह्यत्।
6. सा अवदत् अहम् शूर्पणखा।
7. मम सोदरः रावणः नाम।
8. सः राक्षसानाम् नृपः।

[continued next page]

Rāma refuses Śūrpaṇakhā's request for him to marry her.

[continued from previous page]

9. हे राम तव भार्या भविष्यामि इति।
10. तत् श्रुत्वा रामः अहसत् अवदत् च मम भार्या सीता इति।
11. शूर्पणखा कुपिता भूत्वा सीताम् खादिष्यामि इति अवदत्।
12. लक्ष्मणस्य खड्गेन शूर्पणखायाः नासिका छिन्ना।
13. लक्ष्मणेन शूर्पणखायाः कर्णौ अपि छिन्नौ।
14. रक्तम् सर्वत्र आसीत्।
15. शूर्पणखा रावणम् अधावत्।
16. रावणः शूर्पणखाम् दृष्ट्वा कुपितः अभवत्।
17. रामम् व्यापादयिष्यामि इति रावणः अचिन्तयत्॥

The Forms of मित्रम्

We use मित्रम् as an example of a neuter noun.

SINGULAR	*DUAL*	*PLURAL*
मित्रम् one friend	मित्रे two friends	मित्राणि many friends
हे मित्र O friend	हे मित्रे O two friends	हे मित्राणि O many friends
मित्रम् one friend (2nd)	मित्रे two friends (2nd)	मित्राणि many friends (2nd)
मित्रेण by a friend	मित्राभ्याम् by two friends	मित्रैः by many friends
मित्राय for a friend	मित्राभ्याम् for two friends	मित्रेभ्यः for many friends
मित्रात् from a friend	मित्राभ्याम् from two friends	मित्रेभ्यः from many friends
मित्रस्य of a friend	मित्रयोः of two friends	मित्राणाम् of many friends
मित्रे in a friend	मित्रयोः in two friends	मित्रेषु in many friends

Exercise 27

In your exercise book, translate the following into English. Give all possible translations.

1. मित्रेण
2. मित्राणि
3. नगरस्य
4. पुष्पे
5. पुस्तकाभ्याम्
6. फलस्य
7. द्वारयोः
8. वनैः
9. गृहाणाम्
10. मित्रम्

Exercise 28

In your exercise book, translate the following into Sanskrit.

1. for many friends
2. O two doors
3. water (2nd)
4. of a town
5. in many houses
6. from the forest
7. two fruits
8. by a friend
9. in a book
10. by two ropes

Exercise 29

In your exercise book, translate the following into English. Give all possible translations.

1. रामस्य
2. मित्रम्
3. पुष्पेषु
4. हस्तानाम्
5. नरेभ्यः
6. पुस्तकयोः
7. पुत्राः
8. वनात्
9. गृहे
10. सर्पे

Exercise 30

In your exercise book, translate the following into Sanskrit.

1. from Rāma
2. from two houses
3. in many forests
4. by two kings
5. for the king
6. of the town
7. in the hand
8. for two fruits
9. many doors (2nd)
10. from the ear

Writing Sanskrit with English Letters

Now we shall learn how to write the rest of the Sanskrit alphabet using English letters.

ह	ha	ङ	ṅa
य	ya	ञ	ña
र	ra	ण	ṇa
ल	la	न	na
व	va	म	ma

श śa   ष ṣa   स sa

ं ṁ   ः ḥ

Exercise 31

In your exercise book, write the following Sanskrit letters using English letters.

1. स
2. र
3. ञ
4. य
5. ः
6. श
7. ण
8. व

Exercise 32

In your exercise book, write the following in Sanskrit.

1. ṅa
2. ṁ
3. la
4. na
5. ha
6. sa
7. saḥ
8. ma

Exercise 33

In your exercise book, write the following Sanskrit words using English letters.

1. आगतः
2. एव
3. सः
4. खगः
5. मम
6. सह
7. जनः

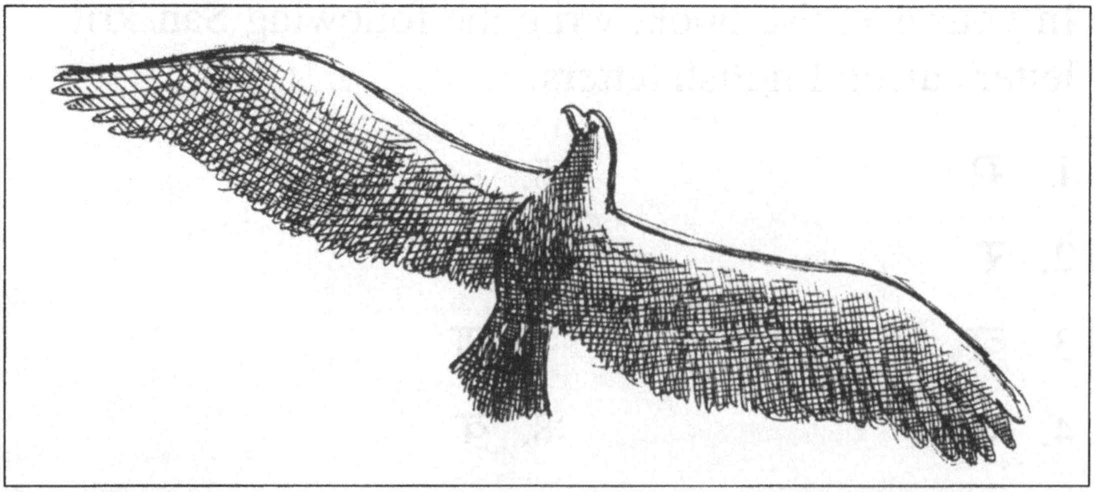

Exercise 34

In your exercise book, write the following in Sanskrit. Then say what each word means. It may help first to write out the English letters and then the equivalent Sanskrit letters underneath.

1. janakaḥ
2. tava
3. na
4. naraḥ
5. bharataḥ
6. rathaḥ
7. śaraḥ
8. saḥ
9. ca

New Words for the Next Story

मारिचः	Mārica	रामवत्	like Rāma
माया	magic	हा हा	alas! alas!
सुवर्ण°	golden	भीत°	afraid
मृगः	deer	सः	that (masculine)
कृत्वा	having made,	स्वरः	voice
	having put on	रक्ष	protect!
आनय	bring!	मुनिजनः	monk
प्रति (+ 2nd)	towards	गृहीत्वा	having grabbed
दूरम्	a long way	पुनः पुनः	again and again

Chapter Six

STORY

Mārīca's Magic Helps Rāvaṇa Kidnap Sītā

Vālmīki says:
"Rāvaṇa's friend, Mārīca, puts on the form of a golden deer. Sītā asks Rāma to bring the deer to her. Rāma pursues the deer, and is drawn away from Sītā. Mārīca, imitating Rāma, cries out for help when he is struck down by Rāma's arrow. Lakṣmaṇa leaves Sītā to help Rāma, and Rāvaṇa, disguised as a monk, comes to Sītā. When Sītā refuses to be his wife, Rāvaṇa takes her away by force."

The story in Sanskrit:

1. रावणस्य मित्रम् मारिचः नाम।
2. मारिचः मायाम् अकरोत्।

[continues on next page]

3. मारीचः सुवर्णस्य मृगस्य रूपम् कृत्वा रामस्य पर्णगृहम् अगच्छत्।

4. सुवर्णम् मृगम् दृष्ट्वा सीता अवदत् हे राम सुवर्णम् मृगम् आनय इति। *[continues on next page]*

Rāvaṇa watches as Sītā asks Rāma to pursue the deer.

[continued from page 55]

5. सीताम् श्रुत्वा रामः सुवर्णम् मृगम् प्रति अधावत्।
6. मारीचः दूरम् अधावत्।
7. मारीचः रामवत् अक्रोशत् हा हा सीते हा हा लक्ष्मण इति।
8. सः रामस्य शरेण हतः।
9. रामस्य स्वरम् श्रुत्वा सीता लक्ष्मणम् अवदत् अहम् भीता ... सः रामस्य स्वरः।
10. हे लक्ष्मण गच्छ रामम् रक्ष इति।
11. लक्ष्मणः रामम् प्रति अधावत्।
12. सर्वम् दृष्ट्वा मुनिजनस्य रूपम् कृत्वा रावणः सीताम् आगच्छत्।

[continues next page]

Rāvaṇa in disguise attracts Sītā's attention.

13. सः अवदत् हे सीते अहम् रावणः नाम।

14. त्वम् मम भार्या भविष्यसि इति।

15. सीता अवदत् न न इति।

16. कुपितः रावणः सीताम् गृहीत्वा पर्णगृहात् अधावत्।

17. सीता पुनः पुनः अक्रोशत् हे राम हे लक्ष्मण इति॥

Rāvaṇa carries off Sītā.

The Forms of सीता

We use सीता as an example of a feminine noun.

SINGULAR	*DUAL*	*PLURAL*
सीता one Sītā	सीते two Sītās	सीताः many Sītās
हे सीते O Sītā	हे सीते O two Sītās	हे सीताः O many Sītās
सीताम् one Sītā (2nd)	सीते two Sītās (2nd)	सीताः many Sītās (2nd)
सीतया by Sītā	सीताभ्याम् by two Sītās	सीताभिः by many Sītās
सीतायै for Sītā	सीताभ्याम् for two Sītās	सीताभ्यः for many Sītās
सीतायाः from Sītā	सीताभ्याम् from two Sītās	सीताभ्यः from many Sītās
सीतायाः of Sītā	सीतयोः of two Sītās	सीतानाम् of many Sītās
सीतायाम् in Sītā	सीतयोः in two Sītās	सीतासु in many Sītās

Exercise 35

In your exercise book, translate the following into English. Give all possible translations.

1. सीतासु
2. भार्यायै
3. मायया
4. नौकाभ्याम्
5. नासिकायाम्
6. तारकयोः
7. कौसल्याम्
8. अयोध्यायाः
9. कन्याभिः
10. हे भार्ये

Exercise 36

In your exercise book, translate the following into Sanskrit.

1. from many stars
2. in the two boats
3. daughter (2nd)
4. by boat
5. from magic
6. of many boats
7. many stars
8. for a wife
9. O Kausalyā
10. two noses

Exercise 37

In your exercise book, translate the following into English. Give all possible translations.

1. रामाय
2. सीताभिः
3. सिंहेषु
4. पुस्तकानि
5. तारकायाम्
6. वृक्षाभ्याम्
7. नौकाभ्यः
8. भार्यासु
9. फलम्
10. नगराणाम्

Exercise 38

In your exercise book, translate the following into Sanskrit.

1. from the two lions
2. by many flowers
3. for many stars
4. many houses
5. from the two boys
6. two towns (2nd)
7. in the boat
8. one daughter
9. O many snakes!
10. of Sītā

Writing Sanskrit with English Letters

We shall now learn how to write Sanskrit consonants and vowels together, using English letters.

Let us say that we want to write के, using English letters. First, we write *k*. Then we add the English form of the letter ए, which is *e*. Thus, using English letters, के is written as *ke*.

Use the following chart as a guide for further exercises.

क ka	का kā
कि ki	की kī
कु ku	कू kū
कृ kṛ	कॄ kṝ
के ke	को ko
कै kai	कौ kau

Exercise 39

In your exercise book, write the following Sanskrit letters using English letters.

1. का
2. जो
3. री
4. नु
5. टे
6. ब
7. शृ
8. ञ

Exercise 40

In your exercise book, write the following in Sanskrit.

1. yau
2. mu
3. pha
4. jhā
5. ha
6. vi
7. kṛ
8. hū

Exercise 41

In your exercise book, write the following Sanskrit words using English letters.

1. अपि
2. इति
3. करोति
4. जटायुः
5. नौका
6. पुरुषः
7. गृहाय

Exercise 42

In your exercise book, write the following in Sanskrit. Then say what each word means. It may help first to write out the English letters and then the equivalent Sanskrit letters underneath.

1. bālakaḥ
2. tārakā
3. nāsikā
4. jananī
5. mārīcaḥ
6. acireṇa
7. gṛhītaḥ
8. kausalyā
9. siṁhaḥ

सह with the Third Ending

सह means 'together with' and is used with a word that has the Third Ending

For example:

नरेण सह	together with a man
सीतया सह	together with Sītā

Exercise 43

- In your exercise book, copy the following.
- Then add the correct endings where indicated.
- Finally, translate into English.

1. नर__ सह
2. पुत्र__ सह
3. सीत__ सह
4. फल__ सह
5. कौसल्य__ सह

Exercise 44

In your exercise book, translate the following into Sanskrit.

1. together with Rāma
2. together with Rāvaṇa
3. together with Sītā
4. together with a friend

New Words for the Next Story

लङ्का	Laṅkā, Rāvaṇa's island
वृद्ध॰	old
जटायुः	Jaṭāyu
त्यज	leave alone!
नाशयति	destroys
पक्षः	wing
भूषणम्	jewel
वानरः	monkey

Chapter Seven

STORY

Rāvaṇa Cuts Off Jaṭāyu's Wings

Vālmīki says:
"Jaṭāyu, an old bird and friend of Rāma, tries to rescue Sītā, but has his wings cut off by Rāvaṇa. Rāvaṇa, with Sītā, continues back to his home in Laṅkā, while Jaṭāyu falls to the ground. Sītā throws down some jewels, which are found on the ground by monkeys."

The story in Sanskrit:

1. रावणः सीतया सह रथेन अगच्छत्।
2. रथः गगने लङ्काम् प्रति अगच्छत्।
3. वृद्धः खगः जटायुः नाम आसीत्।

[continues on next page]

4. सीतायाः स्वरम् श्रुत्वा हे रावण सीताम् त्यज इति सः अक्रोशत्।

5. रावणः न अशृणोत्।

6. जटायुः रावणेन सह युद्धम् अकरोत्।

7. युद्धम् दीर्घम् घोरम् च।

[continues on page 69]

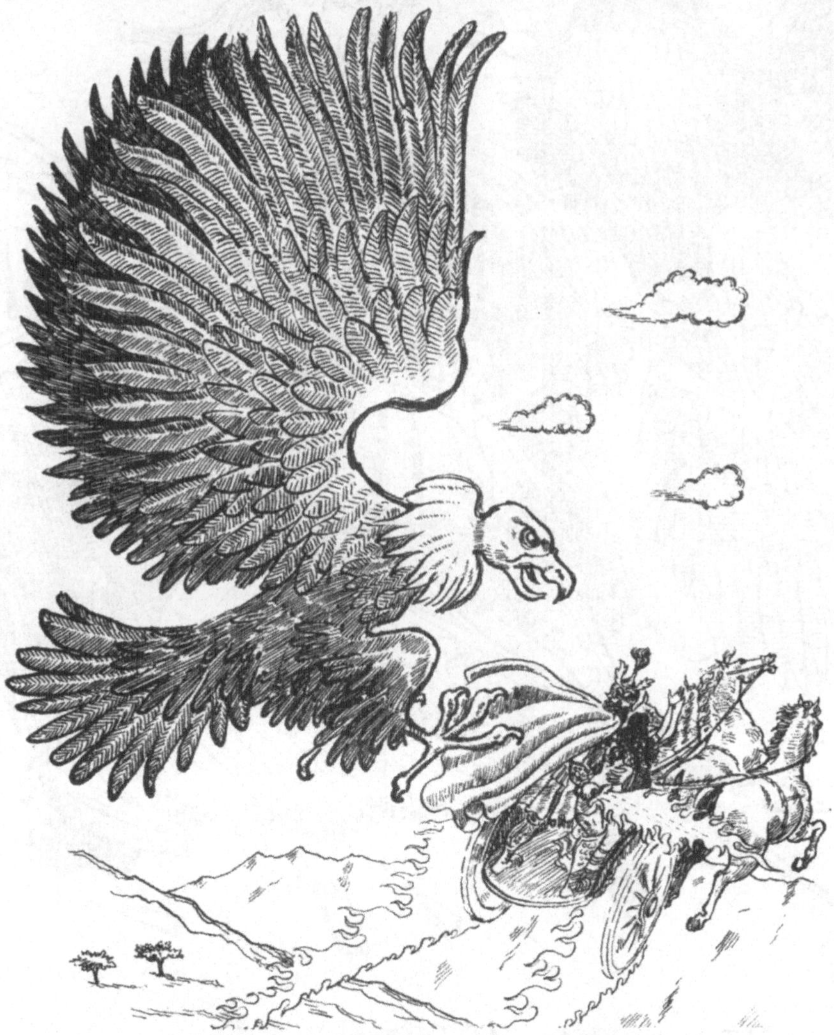

Jaṭāyu challenges Rāvaṇa.

Rāvaṇa cuts off Jaṭāyu's wings.

[continued from page 67]

8. जटायुः रावणस्य रथम् अनाशयत्।
9. रावणेन वृद्धस्य खगस्य पक्षौ छिन्नौ।
10. जटायुः गगनात् भूमिम् अपतत्।
11. सीताम् गृहीत्वा रावणः गगने लङ्काम् प्रति पुनः अगच्छत्।
12. सीता भूषणानि गगनात् भूमिम् अक्षिपत्।
13. भूम्याम् वानराः आसन्।
14. वानराः भूषणानि अपश्यन्।
15. सीतायाः भूषणानि वानरैः गृहीतानि।
16. वानराः सीताम् रावणम् च गगने अपश्यन्॥

The Neuter Forms of तत्

तत् means 'that'. Here are its neuter forms.

SINGULAR	*DUAL*	*PLURAL*
तत् that	ते those two	तानि those many
तत् that (2nd)	ते those two (2nd)	तानि those many (2nd)
तेन by that	ताभ्याम् by those two	तैः by those many
तस्मै for that	ताभ्याम् for those two	तेभ्यः for those many
तस्मात् from that	ताभ्याम् from those two	तेभ्यः from those many
तस्य of that	तयोः of those two	तेषाम् of those many
तस्मिन् in that	तयोः in those two	तेषु in those many

Note to teacher/student: In the dual and plural, 2nd Ending onwards, sometimes तत् *is translated as 'them'.*

Exercise 45

In your exercise book, translate the following into English. Give all possible translations.

1.	तत्	5.	तस्मात्
2.	ताभ्याम्	6.	तेभ्यः
3.	तस्मिन्	7.	तयोः
4.	तेषाम्	8.	ते

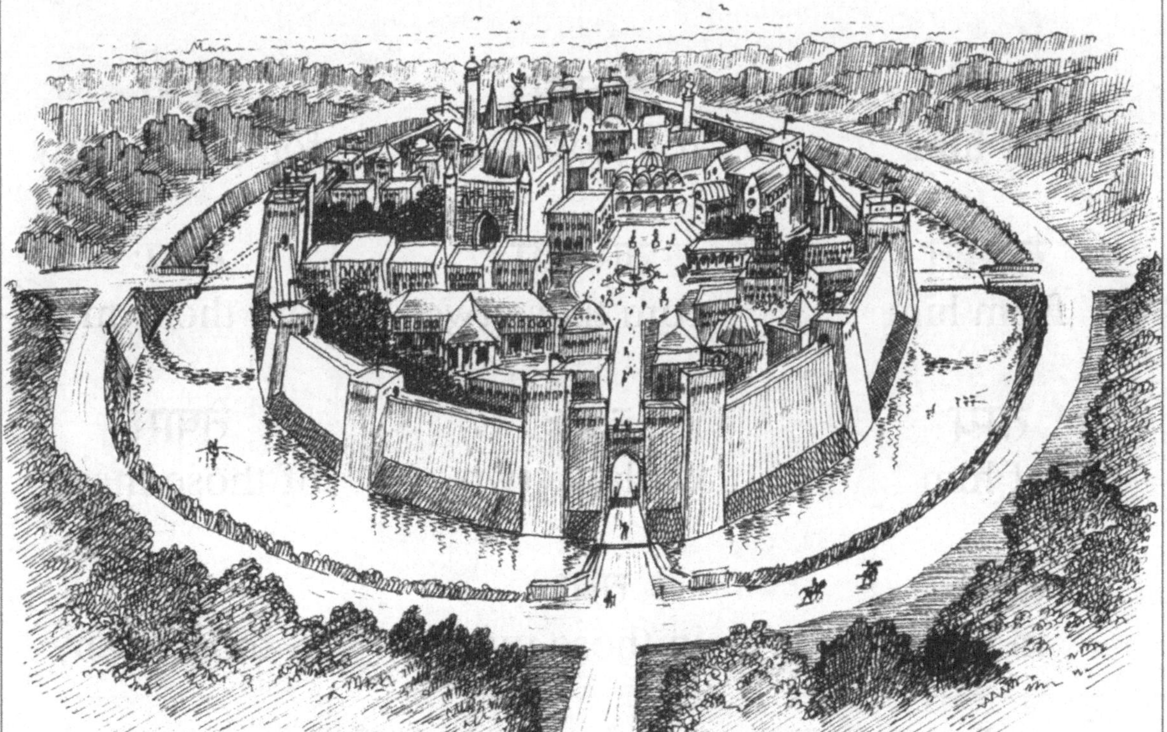

The island of Laṅkā

The Masculine Forms of तत्

Note that सः means 'he'. It can also be used as 'that' with masculine nouns.

SINGULAR	*DUAL*	*PLURAL*
सः he	तौ those two	ते those many
तम् him (2nd)	तौ those two (2nd)	तान् those many (2nd)
तेन by him	ताभ्याम् by those two	तैः by those many
तस्मै for him	ताभ्याम् for those two	तेभ्यः for those many
तस्मात् from him	ताभ्याम् from those two	तेभ्यः from those many
तस्य of him	तयोः of those two	तेषाम् of those many
तस्मिन् in him	तयोः in those two	तेषु in those many

Note to teacher/student: In the dual and plural, 2nd Ending onwards, sometimes तत् *is translated as 'them'.*

Exercise 46

In your exercise book, translate the following into English. Give all possible translations.

1. तत्
2. सः
3. तैः
4. तान्
5. तानि
6. ते
7. तेषु
8. तस्य

Exercise 47

In your exercise book, translate the following into Sanskrit.

1. from them
2. in them
3. he
4. that
5. by that
6. for him

Exercise 48

In your exercise book, translate the following Sanskrit sentences into English. For each sentence:

- first write the Sanskrit;
- then write a word-for-word translation;
- and finally write out a full translation.

1. सः नगरम् अगच्छत्।
2. राक्षसम् तस्मै व्यापादयामि।
3. तस्य रथः अत्र अस्ति।
4. जटायुः तम् पक्षेण अतुदत्।

Exercise 49

In your exercise book, translate the following into Sanskrit.

1. He goes.
2. He goes to the house.
3. I sing for him.
4. The bird hit him with his wing.

तत् Can Also Describe a Noun

Although तत्, सः and all the other forms can be used on their own, they can also be used to describe a noun. For example:

तत् पुस्तकम्	that book
सः नरः	that man
तेन पुस्तकेन	by that book
तम् नरम्	that man (2nd)

Like normal adjectives, तत् and सः must agree with the noun to which they belong.

Exercise 50

In your exercise book, translate the following into English. Give all possible translations.

1. सः वरः
2. सः बालकः
3. तम् वृक्षम्
4. तयोः नगरयोः
5. तानि पुष्पाणि
6. ते नराः
7. तस्मिन् गृहे
8. तान् राक्षसान्
9. तौ चन्द्रौ
10. तस्मै फलाय

Exercise 51

In your exercise book, translate the following into Sanskrit.

1. that king
2. that friend
3. from that forest
4. by those two men
5. that door (2nd)
6. for those many sons
7. those two books
8. those two trees
9. in that water
10. of that boy

Exercise 52

In your exercise book, translate the following Sanskrit sentences into English. For each sentence:

- first write the Sanskrit;
- then write a word-for-word translation;
- and finally write out a full translation.

1. सः नरः वृक्षात् अपतत् ।
2. बालकाः तम् राक्षसम् अतुदन् ।
3. तत् पुष्पम् रुचिरम् अस्ति ।
4. नारी नगरम् तेन रथेन अगच्छत् ।
5. तस्मिन् वने सिंहः कुक्कुरम् खादिष्यति ।

Exercise 53

In your exercise book, translate the following into Sanskrit.

1. That boy eats.
2. That boy eats a fruit.
3. The man goes to town by that elephant.
4. I shall eat that fruit.

Writing Sanskrit with English Letters

So far we have only written consonants joined to vowels. But what happens if we have a halanta letter, like क्?
In this case, all we do is write the English letter without a vowel.

Thus, क् is written as *k*.

Here are some more examples:

क	ka	क्	k
न	na	न्	n
ध	dha	ध्	dh
य	ya	य्	y
श	śa	श्	ś

Exercise 54

In your exercise book, copy this chart and fill it in. The first one is done for you.

Non-Halanta Letters		Halanta Letters	
In Sanskrit	*In English*	*In Sanskrit*	*In English*
ब	ba	ब्	b
त			
झ			
र्			
ष			
ठ			
ङ			

Exercise 55

In your exercise book, write the following in Sanskrit.

1. p
2. g
3. kh
4. tat
5. yat
6. kim
7. ṛk
8. etad
9. phalam
10. cibukam

Exercise 56

In your exercise book, write the following Sanskrit words using English letters.

1. तत्
2. तान्
3. माम्
4. इयम्
5. रामान्
6. वनम्
7. बहुकालम्

New Words for the Next Story

हत्वा	having killed
कुत्र	where ?
मूढवत्	like a fool
पृच्छति	asks
अपहृत°	carried off
उदित्वा	having said
देहः	body
दहति	burns

Chapter Eight

STORY

Rāma, Grieving for Sītā, Finds Jaṭāyu Dying

Vālmīki says:
"Rāma meanwhile, having killed Mārīca, returns to the leaf-house to find Sītā gone. Rāma asks all the creatures of the forest to tell him where Sītā is. He finds Jaṭāyu, who tells him that Rāvaṇa has taken Sītā away. The old bird dies, and Rāma and Lakṣmaṇa burn his body."

The story in Sanskrit:

1. मारीचम् हत्वा रामः पर्णगृहम् प्रति अगच्छत् ।
2. मार्गे तु लक्ष्मणम् दृष्ट्वा कुत्र सीता इति रामः तम् अवदत् ।

[continues on page 82]

Rāma finds Jaṭāyu dying.

[continued from page 80]

3. सीता पर्णगृहे इति लक्ष्मणः अवदत्।
4. पर्णगृहे तु तौ सीताम् न अपश्यताम्।
5. सीताम् न दृष्ट्वा रामः मूढवत् वृक्षान् अपृच्छत्
   कुत्र सीता इति।
6. मृगम् गजम् सिंहम् च दृष्ट्वा कुत्र सीता इति
   सः पुनः पुनः शोकेन अपृच्छत्।

7. अचिरेण रामः लक्ष्मणः च वृद्धम् खगम्
   आगच्छताम्।
8. तस्य खगस्य पक्षौ छिन्नौ।
9. रक्तम् सर्वत्र आसीत्।
10. सः खगः रामम् अवदत् तव सीता रावणेन
    अपहृता इति।
11. तत् उदित्वा जटायुः मृतः अभवत्।
12. रामः लक्ष्मणः च तस्य खगस्य देहम् अदहताम्॥

The Feminine Forms of तत्

Note that सा means 'she'. It can also be used as 'that' with feminine nouns.

SINGULAR	*DUAL*	*PLURAL*
सा she	ते those two	ताः those many
ताम् her (2nd)	ते those two (2nd)	ताः those many (2nd)
तया by her	ताभ्याम् by those two	ताभिः by those many
तस्यै for her	ताभ्याम् for those two	ताभ्यः for those many
तस्याः from her	ताभ्याम् from those two	ताभ्यः from those many
तस्याः of her	तयोः of those two	तासाम् of those many
तस्याम् in her	तयोः in those two	तासु in those many

Note to teacher/student: In the dual and plural, 2nd Ending onwards, sometimes तत् *is translated as 'them'.*

Exercise 57

In your exercise book, translate the following into English. Give all possible translations.

1. सा
2. ताः
3. ताम्
4. ते
5. तस्यै
6. सा नारी
7. तस्याः मायायाः
8. ताभ्याम् नौकाभ्याम्
9. तया कन्यया
10. तासाम् नासिकानाम्

Exercise 58

In your exercise book, translate the following into Sanskrit.

1. in her
2. in those two (fem.)
3. from those two (fem.)
4. by them (fem.)
5. in them (fem.)
6. by that magic
7. those many wives
8. of those two noses
9. that boat (2nd)
10. from that star

Using the 6th Ending to Say 'Have'

In Sanskrit, there is no way of saying you 'have' something.
You cannot say 'The man has a dog.'
Instead, you say '<u>Of</u> the man there is a dog.'
To do this, Sanskrit uses the 6th Ending.
For example:

नरस्य	कुक्कुरः	अस्ति
<u>of</u> the man	a dog	there is

<u>Of</u> the man there is a dog.

The man has a dog.

Another example:

नृपाणाम्	नौकाः	सन्ति
<u>of</u> the kings	ships	there are

<u>Of</u> the kings there are ships.

The kings have ships.

Exercise 59

In your exercise book, translate the following Sanskrit sentences into English. For each sentence:

- first write the Sanskrit;
- then write a word-for-word translation;
- and finally write out a full translation.

1. नरस्य मृगः अस्ति।
2. नरस्य मृगः आसीत्।
3. नृपस्य रथः अस्ति।
4. नृपाणाम् रथाः सन्ति।
5. नृपयोः रथौ स्तः।
6. भार्यायाः पुत्रः अस्ति।
7. भार्याणाम् भूषणानि सन्ति।
8. मित्रयोः फले स्तः।

Exercise 60

In your exercise book, translate the following into Sanskrit.

1. Of the boy there is a monkey.
2. The boy has a dog.
3. Of the daughters there is a father.
4. The daughters have a friend.
5. Of the town there are roads.
6. The town has many trees.

Writing Sanskrit with English Letters

We shall now learn how to write joined consonants, using English letters. We start with the most simple type. Look at the word गत्वा.

The त्व part is made from त् added to व.

So we write the English letter for त्, which is *t*. We then add to that the English letter for व, which is *va*.

Thus त्व is written as *tva* and गत्वा is written as *gatvā*.

Exercise 61

In your exercise book, write the following Sanskrit sounds using English letters.

1. त्व
2. स्व
3. स्त
4. न्म
5. द्ध
6. ङ्क
7. ष्य
8. श्च

Exercise 62

In your exercise book, write the following in Sanskrit.

1. ṣpa
2. ṣṇa
3. ghna
4. tsa
5. tsya
6. ṅka
7. ddh
8. lya

Exercise 63

In your exercise book, write the following Sanskrit words using English letters.

1. अन्तः
2. अल्पः
3. अन्यः
4. अग्निः
5. द्वितीया
6. अयोध्या
7. लङ्का

Exercise 64

In your exercise book, write the following in Sanskrit. Then say what each word means. It may help first to write out the English letters and then the equivalent Sanskrit letters underneath.

1. gatvā
2. dhṛtvā
3. hatvā
4. gacchati
5. cintayati
6. nāśayati
7. vyāpādayati
8. kausalyā
9. dvāram

APPENDICES

		Page
1	Verses to Recite	91
2	Writing Sanskrit with English Letters	94
3	Summary of Word Forms	99
4	Vocabulary: English–Sanskrit	108
5	Vocabulary: Sanskrit–English	117

Appendix 1

Verses to Recite

The following verses can be recited daily, section by section, progressing gradually until known by heart. The verses are taken from the ***Bhagavad Gitā****, in which Kṛṣṇa advises Arjuna, who is about to engage in battle. Kṛṣṇa speaks as God incarnate, hence capital letters are used for 'My' and 'Me' etc.*

Chapter 9: Kṛṣṇa speaks of true devotion.

यत्करोषि यदश्नासि यज्जुहोषि ददासि यत्।
यत्तपस्यसि कौन्तेय तत्कुरुष्व मदर्पणम् ॥ 27 ॥

Whatever you do, whatever you eat, whatever you sacrifice and give, whatever austerities you practise, do it as an offering to Me.

शुभाशुभफलैरेवं मोक्ष्यसे कर्मबन्धनैः।
संन्यासयोगयुक्तात्मा विमुक्तो मामुपैष्यसि ॥ 28 ॥

So shall your action be attended by no result, either good or bad; through the spirit of renunciation you will come to Me.

समोऽहं सर्वभूतेषु न मे द्वेष्योऽस्ति न प्रियः।
ये भजन्ति तु मां भक्त्या मयि ते तेषु चाप्यहम्॥ 29 ॥

The same I am to all beings; to Me there is none hateful or dear; but those who worship Me with devotion, they live in Me, and I in them.

Chapter 3: Kṛṣṇa teaches about how the wise act.

प्रकृतेः क्रियमाणानि गुणैः कर्माणि सर्वशः।
अहङ्कारविमूढात्मा कर्ताऽहमिति मन्यते॥ 27 ॥

Actions are being performed only by the powers of Nature. The ignorant man, deluded by ego, thinks 'I am the doer'.

मयि सर्वाणि कर्माणि संन्यस्याध्यात्मचेतसा।
निराशीर्निर्ममो भूत्वा युध्यस्व विगतज्वरः॥ 30 ॥

Surrendering all actions to Me, with your heart intent on the Self, free from desire and without selfishness, fight and worry not.

ये मे मतमिदं नित्यमनुतिष्ठन्ति मानवाः।
श्रद्धावन्तोऽनसूयन्तो मुच्यन्ते तेऽपि कर्मभिः ॥ 31 ॥

Those who act always according to My law, full of faith and without ill-will, they are freed from the bonds of action.

इन्द्रियस्येन्द्रियस्यार्थे रागद्वेषौ व्यवस्थितौ।
तयोर्न वशमागच्छेत्तौ ह्यस्य परिपन्थिनौ ॥ 34 ॥

Do not yield to the passion and hatred aroused towards the objects of sense. They only obstruct the path of Truth.

श्रेयान्स्वधर्मो विगुणः परधर्मात् स्वनुष्ठितात्।
स्वधर्मे निधनं श्रेयः परधर्मो भयावह ॥ 35 ॥

Better one's own duty, however lacking in merit, than the duty of another, even though well performed. Better is death in one's own duty. To do the duty of another is fraught with danger.

APPENDIX 2

Writing Sanskrit with English Letters

All the texts in this volume that relate to the writing of Sanskrit with English letters are brought together in this Appendix for easy reference.

Vowels

The first rule is that long vowels are written with a bar over them. Thus:

अ	*is written* a	आ	*is written* ā
इ	*is written* i	ई	*is written* ī
उ	*is written* u	ऊ	*is written* ū
ऋ	*is written* ṛ	ॠ	*is written* ṝ

Then we have ए, ऐ, ओ and औ.

ए	*is written* e	ओ	*is written* o
ऐ	*is written* ai	औ	*is written* au

Some Consonants

क	ka	च	ca	ट	ṭa	त	ta	प	pa
ख	kha	छ	cha	ठ	ṭha	थ	tha	फ	pha
ग	ga	ज	ja	ड	ḍa	द	da	ब	ba
घ	gha	झ	jha	ढ	ḍha	ध	dha	भ	bha

The Rest of the Sanskrit Alphabet

ह	ha	ङ	ṅa
य	ya	ञ	ña
र	ra	ण	ṇa
ल	la	न	na
व	va	म	ma

श	śa	ष	ṣa	स	sa
ं	ṁ	ः	ḥ		

Consonants and Vowels Together

Let us say that we want to write के, using English letters. First, we write *k*. Then we add the English form of the letter ए, which is *e*. Thus, using English letters, के is written as *ke*.

Use the following chart as a guide for further exercises.

क ka	का kā
कि ki	की kī
कु ku	कू kū
कृ kṛ	कॄ kṝ
के ke	को ko
कै kai	कौ kau

Halanta Letters

So far we have only written consonants joined to vowels. But what happens if we have a halanta letter, like क्?

In this case, all we do is write the English letter without a vowel.

Thus, क् is written as *k*.

Here are some more examples:

क	ka	क्	k
न	na	न्	n
ध	dha	ध्	dh
य	ya	य्	y
श	śa	श्	ś

Joined Consonants

We start with the most simple type.
Look at the word गत्वा.

The त्व part is made from
त् added to व.

So we write the English letter for त्,
which is *t*. We then add to that the English
letter for व, which is *va*.

Thus त्व is written as *tva* and
गत्वा is written as *gatvā*.

APPENDIX 3

Summary of Word Forms

All the paradigms introduced in 'The Stories of Krishna' (Parts One and Two) and in this first volume of 'The Story of Rāma' are reproduced in this appendix for easy reference.

भवति – All the Present Time Forms

	SINGULAR	DUAL	PLURAL
First Person	भवति he, she, it becomes	भवतः they two become	भवन्ति they many become
Middle Person	भवसि you become	भवथः you two become	भवथ you many become
Best Person	भवामि I become	भवावः we two become	भवामः we many become

The Future Time of भवति

	SINGULAR	*DUAL*	*PLURAL*
First Person	भविष्यति he, she, it will become	भविष्यतः they two will become	भविष्यन्ति they many will become
Middle Person	भविष्यसि you will become	भविष्यथः you two will become	भविष्यथ you many will become
Best Person	भविष्यामि I shall become	भविष्यावः we two shall become	भविष्यामः we many shall become

The Past Time of भवति

	SINGULAR	*DUAL*	*PLURAL*
First Person	अभवत् he, she, it became	अभवताम् they two became	अभवन् they many became
Middle Person	अभवः you became	अभवतम् you two became	अभवत you many became
Best Person	अभवम् I became	अभवाव we two became	अभवाम we many became

All the Forms of रामः

We use रामः as an example of a masculine noun ending in -अः.

SINGULAR	*DUAL*	*PLURAL*
रामः one Rāma	रामौ two Rāmas	रामाः many Rāmas
हे राम O Rāma	हे रामौ O two Rāmas	हे रामाः O many Rāmas
रामम् Rāma (2nd)	रामौ two Rāmas (2nd)	रामान् many Rāmas (2nd)
रामेण by Rāma	रामाभ्याम् by two Rāmas	रामैः by many Rāmas
रामाय for Rāma	रामाभ्याम् for two Rāmas	रामेभ्यः for many Rāmas
रामात् from Rāma	रामाभ्याम् from two Rāmas	रामेभ्यः from many Rāmas
रामस्य of Rāma	रामयोः of two Rāmas	रामाणाम् of many Rāmas
रामे in Rāma	रामयोः in two Rāmas	रामेषु in many Rāmas

The Endings for All Masculines in -अः

Like रामः, here is another example, शरः, 'arrow', of the endings used with all masculine nouns ending in -अः.

SINGULAR	*DUAL*	*PLURAL*
शरः one arrow	शरौ two arrows	शराः many arrows
हे शर O arrow	हे शरौ O two arrows	हे शराः O many arrows
शरम् arrow (2nd)	शरौ two arrows (2nd)	शरान् many arrows (2nd)
शरेण by an arrow	शराभ्याम् by two arrows	शरैः by many arrows
शराय for an arrow	शराभ्याम् for two arrows	शरेभ्यः for many arrows
शरात् from an arrow	शराभ्याम् from two arrows	शरेभ्यः from many arrows
शरस्य of an arrow	शरयोः of two arrows	शराणाम् of many arrows
शरे in an arrow	शरयोः in two arrows	शरेषु in many arrows

The Forms of मित्रम्

We use मित्रम् as an example of a neuter noun.

SINGULAR	*DUAL*	*PLURAL*
मित्रम् one friend	मित्रे two friends	मित्राणि many friends
हे मित्र O friend	हे मित्रे O two friends	हे मित्राणि O many friends
मित्रम् one friend (2nd)	मित्रे two friends (2nd)	मित्राणि many friends (2nd)
मित्रेण by a friend	मित्राभ्याम् by two friends	मित्रैः by many friends
मित्राय for a friend	मित्राभ्याम् for two friends	मित्रेभ्यः for many friends
मित्रात् from a friend	मित्राभ्याम् from two friends	मित्रेभ्यः from many friends
मित्रस्य of a friend	मित्रयोः of two friends	मित्राणाम् of many friends
मित्रे in a friend	मित्रयोः in two friends	मित्रेषु in many friends

The Forms of सीता

We use सीता as an example of a feminine noun.

SINGULAR	*DUAL*	*PLURAL*
सीता one Sītā	सीते two Sītās	सीताः many Sītās
हे सीते O Sītā	हे सीते O two Sītās	हे सीताः O many Sītās
सीताम् one Sītā (2nd)	सीते two Sītās (2nd)	सीताः many Sītās (2nd)
सीतया by Sītā	सीताभ्याम् by two Sītās	सीताभिः by many Sītās
सीतायै for Sītā	सीताभ्याम् for two Sītās	सीताभ्यः for many Sītās
सीतायाः from Sītā	सीताभ्याम् from two Sītās	सीताभ्यः from many Sītās
सीतायाः of Sītā	सीतयोः of two Sītās	सीतानाम् of many Sītās
सीतायाम् in Sītā	सीतयोः in two Sītās	सीतासु in many Sītās

The Neuter Forms of तत्

तत् means 'that'. Here are its neuter forms.

SINGULAR	*DUAL*	*PLURAL*
तत् that	ते those two	तानि those many
तत् that (2nd)	ते those two (2nd)	तानि those many (2nd)
तेन by that	ताभ्याम् by those two	तैः by those many
तस्मै for that	ताभ्याम् for those two	तेभ्यः for those many
तस्मात् from that	ताभ्याम् from those two	तेभ्यः from those many
तस्य of that	तयोः of those two	तेषाम् of those many
तस्मिन् in that	तयोः in those two	तेषु in those many

Note to teacher/student: In the dual and plural, 2nd Ending onwards, sometimes तत् *is translated as 'them'.*

The Masculine Forms of तत्

Note that सः means 'he'. It can also be used as 'that' with masculine nouns.

SINGULAR	*DUAL*	*PLURAL*
सः he	तौ those two	ते those many
तम् him (2nd)	तौ those two (2nd)	तान् those many (2nd)
तेन by him	ताभ्याम् by those two	तैः by those many
तस्मै for him	ताभ्याम् for those two	तेभ्यः for those many
तस्मात् from him	ताभ्याम् from those two	तेभ्यः from those many
तस्य of him	तयोः of those two	तेषाम् of those many
तस्मिन् in him	तयोः in those two	तेषु in those many

Note to teacher/student: In the dual and plural, 2nd Ending onwards, sometimes तत् *is translated as 'them'.*

The Feminine Forms of तत्

Note that सा means 'she'. It can also be used as 'that' with feminine nouns.

SINGULAR	*DUAL*	*PLURAL*
सा she	ते those two	ताः those many
ताम् her (2nd)	ते those two (2nd)	ताः those many (2nd)
तया by her	ताभ्याम् by those two	ताभिः by those many
तस्यै for her	ताभ्याम् for those two	ताभ्यः for those many
तस्याः from her	ताभ्याम् from those two	ताभ्यः from those many
तस्याः of her	तयोः of those two	तासाम् of those many
तस्याम् in her	तयोः in those two	तासु in those many

Note to teacher/student: In the dual and plural, 2nd Ending onwards, sometimes तत् is translated as 'them'.

APPENDIX 4

Vocabulary: English – Sanskrit

This English–Sanskrit vocabulary comprises in alphabetical order the appropriate English renderings of all the Sanskrit words used in the exercises, games and stories found in the two volumes of 'The Stories of Krishna' and in this first volume of 'The Story of Rāma'.

A

afraid	भीत°
again	पुनः
again and again	पुनः पुनः
Agha, name of a demon	अघः
alas! alas!	हा हा
alone, only	एव (emphasises previous word)
also	अपि
and	च
angry	कुपित°
are – they two are	स्तः
– they many are	सन्ति
Arjuna	अर्जुनः
arrow	शरः
as if, like	इव
asked	अपृच्छत्
asks	पृच्छति
asks for	प्रार्थयति
ate	अखादत्
Ayodhyā	अयोध्या

B

battle	युद्धम्
beautiful	रमणीय°, रुचिर°
became	अभवत्
(having) become	भूत्वा
becomes	भवति
best	उत्तम°
Bharata	भरतः
Bhīma	भीमः

binds	बध्नाति
bird	खगः
black	कृष्ण॰
bliss	आनन्दः
blood	रक्तम्
blue	नील॰
boat	नौका
body	देहः
book	पुस्तकम्
bow *[the noun]*	चापः
(having) bowed	नत्वा
bows *[the verb]*	नमति
boy	बालकः
brave	वीर॰
breast	स्तनः
bring!	आनय
brother	सोदरः
built	अकरोत्
burned	अदहत्
burns	दहति
but	तु
butter	नवनीतम्

C

calf	वत्सः
came	आगच्छत्
Cāṇūra	चाणूरः
carried off	अपहृत॰
cave	गुहा
chair	पीठम्
chariot	रथः
chin	चिबुकम्
city	नगरम्
climbs	आरोहति
closes (the eyes)	निमिषति
cloud	मेघः
colour	वर्णः
come	आगत॰
comes	आगच्छति
conquers, is victorious	जयति
cowherd	गोपालः
Creator, the	पितामहः
cried out	अक्रोशत्
cries out	क्रोशति

D

Daśaratha	दशरथः
daughter	कन्या
dead	मृत॰
deer	मृगः
demon	राक्षसः
demoness	राक्षसी
destroyed	अनाशयत्
destroys	नाशयति
did, made	अकरोत्
does, makes	करोति
(having) done	कृत्वा
dog	कुक्कुरः
door	द्वारम्
drank	अपिबत्
drinks	पिबति

E

ear	कर्णः
eats	खादति
elephant	गजः
enters	प्रविशति
everything	सर्वम्
everywhere	सर्वत्र
evil	असाधु॰

F

falls	पतति
falls in love	स्निह्यति (+7th)
far away	दूरे
father	जनकः
fearless	अभय॰
fell	अपतत्
fell in love	अस्निह्यत् (+7th)
fire	अग्निः
first	प्रथम॰
fish	मत्स्यः
flower	पुष्पम्
flute	वंशः
(like a) fool	मूढवत्
forest	वनम्
form	रूपम्
freed	मुक्त॰
friend	मित्रम्

fruit	फलम्

G

gave	अददात्
gives	ददाति
go!	गच्छ
goes	गच्छति
golden	सुवर्ण॰
(having) gone	गत्वा
grabbed	गृहीत॰
(having) grabbed	गृहीत्वा
green	हरित॰
grief	शोकः
ground	भूमिम् (2nd)
(on the) ground	भूम्याम् (7th)

H

hair	केशः
hand	हस्तः
happy	सुखित॰
he	सः
(having) heard	श्रुत्वा
hears	शृणोति
heart	हृदयम्
her, of her	तस्याः
here	अत्र
hidden	तिरोहित॰
him (2nd)	तम्
his, of him	तस्य
hits	तुदति
horrible	घोर॰
house	गृहम्

I

I	अहम्
if	यदि
Indra	इन्द्रः
inside	अन्तः
is	अस्ति

J

Jaṭāyu	जटायुः
Janaka	जनकः
jewel	भूषणम्

jump	प्लवनम्

K

Kaṁsa	कंसः
Kāliya, a serpent demon	कालियः
kills	व्यापादयति
killed	हत॰
(having) killed	हत्वा
king	नृपः
Kubera, the god of wealth	कुबेरः
Kṛṣṇa	कृष्णः
Kaikeyī	कैकेयी
Kausalyā	कौसल्या

L

Lakṣmaṇa	लक्ष्मणः
Laṅkā, Rāvaṇa's island	लङ्का
lady	नारी
large	विशाल॰
laughed	अहसत्
laughs	हसति
leads	नयति
leaf-house	पर्णगृहम्
leave alone!	त्यज
lifted up	उदहरत्
lifts, lifts up	उद्धरति
like, as if	इव
like a fool	मूढवत्
like Rāma	रामवत्
limitless	अनन्त॰
lion	सिंहः
listened	अशृणोत्
long	दीर्घ॰
long ago	पुरा
(for a) long time	बहुकालम्
Lord, the	गोविन्दः

M

made, did	अकरोत्
magic	माया
makes, does	करोति
man	नरः
many	बहु॰

Mārīca	मारीचः
meets	मिलति
(in the) middle	मध्ये
Mithilā	मिथिला
monk	मुनिजनः
monkey	वानरः
moon	चन्द्रः
mother	जननी
mountain	अचलः
mouth	आस्यम्
my	मम

N

name, by name	नाम
Nārada, a sage	नारदः
nose	नासिका
not	न
nowhere	न कुत्रचित्

O

O!	हे
old	वृद्ध°
O my!	अहो
once	एकदा
only, alone (emphasises previous word)	एव
orange	नारङ्ग°
other, another	अन्य°

P

palace	राजगृहम्
person	पुरुषः
person	जनः
pillar	स्तम्भः
plays (an instrument)	वादयति
poison	विशम्
prince	राजपुत्रः
protect!	रक्ष
proud	गर्वित°
pupil	शिष्यः
pure	शुद्ध°
Pūtanā, a demoness	पूतना
(having) put on	कृत्वा

R

rains	वर्षाः
Rāma	रामः
ran	अधावत्
Rāvaṇa	रावणः
red	अरुण॰
river	नदी
road	मार्गः
rope	सूत्रम्
runs	धावति

S

said, spoke	अवदत्
(having) said	उदित्वा
sang	अगायत्
Śatrughna	शत्रुघ्नः
saved	रक्षित॰
saw	अपश्यत्
says	वदति
second	द्वितीय॰
(having) seen	दृष्ट्वा
sees	पश्यति
serpent demon	कालियः
she	सा
shines	भाति
shoots	क्षिपति
short	ह्रस्व॰
silently	तूष्णीम्
sings	गायति
Sītā	सीता
sits down	उपविशति
Śiva	शिवः
Sumitrā	सुमित्रा
Śūrpanakhā	शूर्पनखा
sky	गगनम्
small	अल्प॰
(with a) smile	सस्मितम्
snake	सर्पः
son	पुत्रः
soon	अचिरेण
sound	शब्दः
speaks	वदति
stands	तिष्ठति
star	तारका
stop!	उपरम
stops	उपरमति

strong	प्रबल॰	throat	कण्ठः
sun	सूर्यः	throws	क्षिपति
Supreme Lord, the	परमेश्वरः	'thus' (see p. 11)	इति
		together with	सह (+ 3rd)
sword	खड्गः	towards (used after a 2nd-case word)	प्रति
		town	नगरम्
		tree	वृक्षः

T

teacher	आचार्यः
that	तत् (neuter)
	सः (masc.)
	सा (fem.)
that, him (2nd)	तम् (masc.)
then	तदा
there	तत्र
there is	अस्ति
therefore	तस्मात्
they (two) are	स्तः
thinks	चिन्तयति
(he, she) thought	अचिन्तयत्
three (fem.)	तिस्रः
threw	अक्षिपत्

V

(is) victorious	जयति
Viśvāmitra	विश्वामित्रः
voice	स्वरः

W

walked	अचरत्
walks	चरति
was	आसीत्
water	जलम्
went	अगच्छत्
(they) were	आसन्

what?	किम्
where?	कुत्र
Whirlwind demon, the	चक्रवातः
wife	भार्या
wing	पक्षः
wise	प्राज्ञ॰
wish	वरः
with, together with	सह (+ 3rd)
wood, forest	वनम्
writes	लिखति

Y

Yaśodā	यशोदा
yellow	पीत॰
you	त्वम्
your	तव

APPENDIX 5

Vocabulary: Sanskrit – English

The following vocabulary comprises in alphabetical order all the Sanskrit words, with their appropriate English renderings, used in the exercises, games and stories found in the two volumes of 'The Stories of Krishna' and in this first volume of 'The Story of Rāma'.

अ

अकरोत्	made, did, built
अक्रोशत्	cried out
अक्षिपत्	threw
अखादत्	ate
अगच्छत्	went
अगायत्	sang
अग्निः	fire
अघः	Agha, name of a demon
अचरत्	walked
अचलः	mountain
अचिन्तयत्	thought
अचिरेण	soon
अतुदत्	hit
अत्र	here
अददात्	gave
अदहत्	burned
अधावत्	ran
अनन्त॰	limitless
अन्तः	inside
अनाशयत्	destroyed
अन्य॰	other, another
अपतत्	fell
अपश्यत्	saw
अपहृत॰	carried off
अपृच्छत्	asked
अपि	also
अपिबत्	drank
अभय॰	fearless
अभवत्	became
अयोध्या	Ayodhyā
अरुण॰	red
अर्जुनः	Arjuna
अल्प॰	small

अवदत्	said
अशृणोत्	listened
असाधु°	evil
अस्ति	is
अस्निह्यत्	fell in love
अहम्	I
अहसत्	laughed
अहो	O my!

आ

आगच्छत्	came
आगच्छति	comes
आगत°	come
आचार्यः	teacher
आनन्दः	bliss
आनय	bring!
आरोहति	climbs
आसन्	they were
आसीत्	was
आस्यम्	mouth

इ

इति	'thus' (see p. 11)
इन्द्रः	Indra
इव	like, as if

उ

उत्तम°	best
उदहरत्	lifted, lifted up
उदित्वा	having said
उद्धरति	lifts, lifts up
उपरम	stop!
उपरमति	stops
उपविशति	sits down

ए

एकदा	once
एव	alone, only (emphasises previous word)

क

कण्ठः	throat
कन्या	daughter
कर्णः	ear
करोति	does, makes
कंसः	Kaṁsa
कालियः	Kāliya, a serpent demon

किम्	what?
कुक्कुरः	dog
कुत्र	where?
कुपित°	angry
कुबेरः	Kubera, the god of wealth
कृत्वा	having done, having put on
कृष्ण°	black
कृष्णः	Kṛṣṇa
केशः	hair
कैकेयी	Kaikeyī
कौसल्या	Kausalyā
क्रोशति	cries out
क्षिपति	throws, shoots

ख

खगः	bird
खड्गः	sword
खादति	eats

ग

गगनम्	sky
गच्छ	go!
गच्छति	goes
गजः	elephant
गत्वा	having gone
गमिष्यति	will go
गर्वित°	proud
गायति	sings
गुहा	cave
गृहम्	house
गृहीत°	grabbed
गृहीत्वा	having grabbed
गोपालः	cowherd
गोविन्दः	the Lord

घ

घोर°	horrible

च

च	and
चक्रवातः	the Whirlwind demon
चन्द्रः	moon

चरति	walks
चाणूरः	Cāṇūra
चापः	bow
चिन्तयति	thinks
चिबुकम्	chin

छ

छिन्न॰	cut

ज

जटायुः	Jaṭāyu
जनः	person
जनकः	Janaka
जनकः	father
जननी	mother
जयति	is victorious
जलम्	water

त

तत्	that
तत्र	there
तदा	then
तम्	that, him (2nd)
तव	your
तस्मात्	therefore
तस्य	his
तस्याः	her, of her
ताटका	Tāṭakā
तारका	star
तिरोहित॰	hidden
तिष्ठति	stands
तिस्रः	three (fem.)
तु	but
तुदति	hits
तूष्णीम्	silent
त्यज	leave alone!
त्वम्	you

द

ददाति	gives
दशरथः	Daśaratha
दहति	burns
दीर्घ॰	long
दूरम्	a long way

दूरे	far away
दृष्ट्वा	having seen
देहः	body
द्वारम्	door
द्वितीय°	second

ध

धावति	runs

न

न	not
न कुत्रचित्	nowhere
नगरम्	town, city
नत्वा	having bowed
नदी	river
नमति	bows
नयति	leads
नरः	man
नव°	new
नवनीतम्	butter
नाम	a name, by name
नारङ्ग°	orange
नारदः	Nārada, a sage
नारी	lady
नाशयति	destroys
नासिका	nose
निमिषति	closes the eyes
नील°	blue
नृपः	king
नौका	boat

प

पक्षः	wing
पतति	falls
परमेश्वरः	the Supreme Lord
पर्णगृहम्	leaf-house
पश्यति	sees
पितामहः	the Creator
पिबति	drinks
पीठम्	chair
पीत°	yellow
पुत्रः	son

पुनः	again
पुनः पुनः	again and again
पुरा	long ago
पुरुषः	person
पुष्पम्	flower
पुस्तकम्	book
पूतना	Pūtanā, a demoness
पृच्छति	asks
प्रति	towards (+ 2nd)
प्रथम°	first
प्रबल°	strong
प्रविशति	enters
प्राज्ञ°	wise
प्रार्थयति	asks for
प्लवनम्	a jump

फ

फलम्	fruit

ब

बध्नाति	binds
बहु°	many
बहुकालम्	for a long time
बालकः	boy

भ

भरतः	Bharata
भवति	becomes
भाति	shines
भार्या	wife
भीत°	afraid
भीमः	Bhīma
भूत्वा	having become
भूमिम्	ground (2nd)
भूम्याम्	on the ground
भूषणम्	jewel

म

मत्स्यः	fish
मध्ये	in the middle
मम	my
मारीचः	Mārīca
मार्गः	road
माया	magic

मित्रम्	friend
मिथिला	Mithilā (a city)
मिलति	meets
मुक्त°	freed
मुनिजनः	monk
मूढवत्	like a fool
मृत°	dead
मृगः	deer
मेघः	cloud

य

यदि	if
यशोदा	Yaśodā
युद्धम्	battle

र

रक्तम्	blood
रक्ष	protect!
रक्षित°	saved
रथः	chariot
रमणीय°	beautiful
राक्षसः	demon
राक्षसी	demoness
राजगृहम्	palace
राजपुत्रः	prince
रामः	Rāma
रामवत्	like Rāma
रावणः	Rāvaṇa, king of the demons
रुचिर°	beautiful
रूपम्	form

ल

लक्ष्मणः	Lakṣmaṇa
लङ्का	Laṅkā, Rāvaṇa's island
लिखति	writes

व

वत्सः	calf
वदति	speaks
वनम्	forest
वरः	wish
वर्णः	colour
वर्षाः	rains
वंशः	flute

वादयति	plays (an instrument)
वानरः	monkey
विशम्	poison
विशाल°	large
विश्वामित्रः	Viśvāmitra
विसर्गः	a release of the breath, shown by ः, as in रामः
वीर°	brave
वृक्षः	tree
वृद्ध°	old
व्यापादयति	kills

श

शत्रुघ्नः	Śatrughna
शप्त°	cursed
शब्दः	sound
शरः	arrow
शिवः	Śiva
शिष्यः	pupil
शुद्ध°	pure
शूर्पनखा	Śūrpanakhā
शृणोति	hears
शोकः	grief
श्रुत्वा	having heard

स

सन्ति	they (many) are
सर्पः	snake
सर्वत्र	everywhere
सर्वम्	everything
सस्मितम्	with a smile
सह (+ 3rd)	together with
सः	he
सा	she
सिंहः	lion
सीता	Sītā
सुखित°	happy
सुमित्रा	Sumitrā
सुवर्ण°	golden
सूत्रम्	rope, string
सूर्यः	sun
सोदरः	brother
स्तनः	breast

स्तम्भः	pillar
स्तः	they (two) are
स्निह्यति (+7th)	falls in love
स्वरः	voice

ह

हत॰	killed
हत्वा	having killed
हरित॰	green
हसति	laughs
हस्तः	hand
हा हा	alas! alas!
हृदयम्	heart
हे	O!
ह्रस्व॰	short